# Finding T :
# The Great
# Alphabet Hunt

## Paula Curtis Taylorson

illustrated by Zaida Montes

Finding T : The Great Alphabet Hunt



Printed in the United States of America

A 2 Z Press LLC

PO Box 582

Deleon Springs, FL 32130

bestlittleonlinebookstore.com

sizemore3630@aol.com

440-241-3126

ISBN: 978-1-954191-21-1

## Dedication

*Thank you to those
who read to me and
those who listened
to me read.*

This book
belongs to
TOY

He's a **tense** and **tidy** teacher,
but he's **trusted** and he's **tall**.
Mr. **Terrance Thornton-Tyler** could be
heard from **the** end of **the** hall!

His classes are **terrific**, his lessons **typically topical** and cool.

So, let's **try to** find **the timeless** T words **that** are hiding in his school.

In **the teeny** carpark, **the traffic's** very busy,
there's a **tram**, a **tractor** and a **tank**,

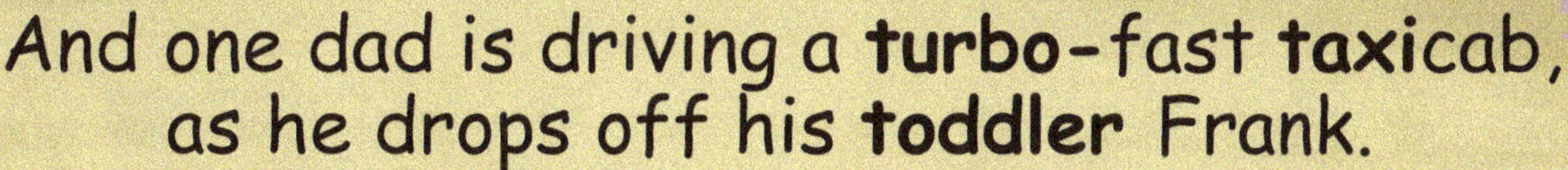

And one dad is driving a **turbo**-fast **taxi**cab,
as he drops off his **toddler** Frank.

Kids **travel** to school on
**tugboats** and **tankers**,
and even by **trucks** with a **trailer**,

While Mr. **Toad** sees **Todd** drop the **tadpoles** by his **tricycle**, on his way **to** his work as a **tailor**.

There's a **timid** girl in a **tutu**, a **trendy** boy in a **tracksuit** and another in a **top** hat and **tails**,

And **Tilly** is **talking to** a **turkey** called Trevor, who is **texting** and sending emails.

Children line up **two** by **two**, **together**
**they** listen for **their** names in roll-call,

**Theo** dresses up as a **tiger**.
He has a **terrifying** roar,
but says nothing at all!

Toby and Tao, the Taiwanese twins, head to their Taekwondo class in room twenty,

Where **they tie** up **their tote** bags
and **take** off **their** coats; making use of **the**
lockers **that** are empty.

'Where is **the toilet** please?'
asks a **tiny** girl with ringlets
and **tubular** curls.

A **tardy** boy with a **toucan** points **to** a sign, 'This way **to the** bathroom for GIRLS!'

Some children sit side by side at **tables**,
**taking turns** reading tales from a book.

They **turn the** pages and read **true** stories
about a pirate **they** call Captain Hook.

The children are taught to **taught** to tell time
on a clock. **Two** o'clock, **three** o'clock, four...

Then tired, they listen to the tick-tock during nap **time** as **they** all lay on mats on **the** floor.

In math **they** count **to** a **thousand** and
do **take-away** and multiply sums.

Using brick **towers to** help add up **the totals,**
and sometimes **they** use **their** fingers and **thumbs.**

Thomas is a **teenage** boy who
carries a **tarantula tucked** in
his **trouser** pocket,

He likes to **tell tales** of how he once **tackled** dragons and **toured** space in a **tip-top** rocket.

Tucked away in **the tuneful** corner, is
a **tortoise** who plays the **trombone**.

And a **tapir** playing
a **timpani** drum with a **tree
frog** on an old **telephone**.

In a **triangular** fish **tank** in the corner, swims a **tuna**, a **turbot** and a **trout**.

And **the teacher's** aide sits on a **tournado toboggan**, while **the teddy** bears march in and out.

At **twelve** o'clock it is lunchtime at last.
Pupils are **tempted** by **the** smells
and **the tastes** of **tomatoes** on
**toast, tacos** with meat,
and **tofu** with **tandoori** paste.

There are **take-away treats** of **tangerines**,
**tiramisu** and **tapioca** with **tahini** and spice.
There's **tap** water, **tea** or **tropical** juice with
a straw and served over crushed ice.

The **timetable** says art and with **their tabards** on,
**they** use **tan**, **turquoise** and **teal** (which is green)
As a girl from **Tahiti** paints a **Texan** cowboy and
a **thoroughbred** horse in a stream.

Mr. **Thornton-Tyler** **taps** away on a **typewriter, typing** a letter **to** a parent called Neville. He **typed,** 'At recess **Thomas** climbed a **tree to the top,'** and **teased** -'that little **Tasmanian Devil!"**

The talent in **this** school is **tremendous**. We give thanks for all **the** things **that** we learn.

Trying to track down **the T** words
is **tricky**. We're sure to find
more **turning** up **the** next **term!**

# My Very Own 'T' Words:

# Glossary

Page 1. **Tense** : nervous, firm
**Tidy** : neat, orderly, good, acceptable
**Teacher** : one who instructs, gives information for learning
**Trusted** : reliance on the integrity, strength,
ability, surety of a person or thing, confidence
**Tall** : having a relatively great height
**Mr. Terrance Thornton-Tyler** : a man or boy's name
**The** : used to refer to something or someone
specifying or particularly

Page 2. **Terrific** : extraordinarily great or intense:
*terrific speed.*, extremely good; wonderful
**Typically** : conforming to a particular type, a certain way
**Topical** : relating to, dealing with matters of current or local interest,
a particular thing. Also on page 2 ; **Tyrannosaurus Rex** : a dinosaur

Page 3. **Try** : to attempt to do or accomplish something
**To** : used for expressing motion or direction toward a point, person,
place, or thing approached and reached, as opposed to *from*
**T** : a letter of the alphabet
**That** : used to indicate a person, thing, idea, state,
event, time, remark pointed out or present

Page 4. **Teeny** : very small
**Traffic** : the movement of vehicles, ships, or persons in an
area, along a street, through an air lane, or over a water route
**There's** : a contracted word for there is
**Tram** : a British streetcar
**Tractor** : a powerful motor-driven vehicle with large, heavy treads,
used for pulling farm machinery or other vehicles,
**Tank** : for here - an armored, self-propelled combat vehicle, armed
with cannon and machine guns and moving on a caterpillar tread

Page 5. **Turbo** : an automobile powered by an internal-combustion engine equipped with a turbocharger
**Taxi**cab : a public passenger vehicle, especially an automobile, usually fitted with a meter for payment
**Toddler** : a young child

Page 6. **Travel** : to go from one place to another by car, train, plane, or ship, take a trip; journey
**Tugboats** : a small, powerful boat for towing or pushing ships, barges, and other water vessels
**Tankers** : a ship, airplane, or truck designed for bulk shipment of liquids or gases
**Trucks** : any of various forms of vehicles for carrying goods and materials
**Trailer** : a large van or wagon drawn by an automobile, truck, or tractor, used especially in hauling animals or objects

Page 7. Mr. **Toad** : a pretend name for a toad
**Todd** : a boy or man's name
**Tadpoles** : the immature form of frogs and toads found in the water
**Tricycle** : a vehicle, especially one for children, having one large front wheel and two small rear wheels, propelled by foot pedals
**Tailor** : a person whose occupation is the making, mending, or altering of clothes, especially suits, coats, and other outer garments

Page 8. **Timid** : shy
**Tutu** : a short, full skirt, usually made of several layers of tarlatan or tulle, worn by ballerinas
**Trendy** : following the latest fashion – clothes
**Tracksuit** : clothing worn by runners
**Top** hat: a big hat
**Tails** : dress clothes with long fabric in the back

Page 9. **Tilly** : a girl or woman's name
**Talking** : to communicate or exchange ideas or information by speaking
**Turkey** : a large bird
**Trevor** : a boy or man's name
**Texting** : digital, written communication with words and symbols

Page 10. **Two** by **two** : the number two
**Together** : into or in union, proximity, contact, or collision, as two or more things
**They** : people in general
**Their** : a form of the possessive case of plural, used as an attributive adjective, before a noun

Page 11. **Theo** : a boy or man's name
**Tiger** : a large wild cat with stripes
**Terrifying** : to cause extreme fear

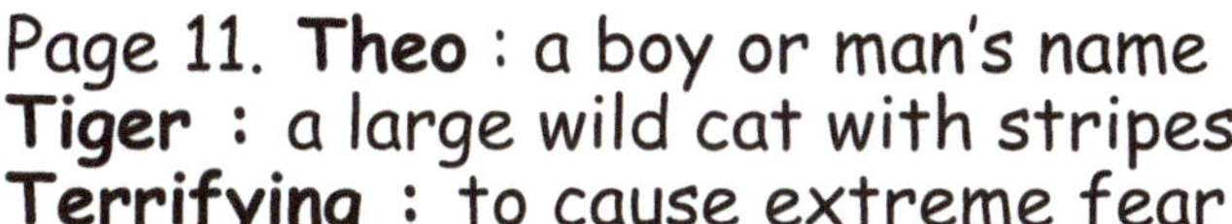

Page 12. **Toby** : a boy or man's name
**Tao** : a boy or man's name
**Taiwanese** : a person from the country of Taiwan
**Twins** : either of two persons or things closely related to or closely resembling each other
**Taekwondo class** : a martial art
**Twenty** : a number

Page 13. **Tie** : to bind, fasten, or attach with a cord, string, or the like, drawn together and knotted
**Tote** bags : an open handbag or shopping bag used especially for carrying packages or small items.
**Take** off : to remove

Page 14. **Toilet** : a bathroom
**Tiny** : very small
**Tubular** : having the shape of a tube, round

Page 15. **Tardy** : late
**Toucan** : a colorful bird
**This** : used to indicate a person, thing, idea, state, event,
time, or remark as present, near, just mentioned or
pointed out, supposed to be understood, or by way of emphasis

Page 16. **Tables** : furniture to place things on
**Taking** : to get into one's hold or possession by voluntary action
**Turns** : each child participates, one at a time

Page 17. **Turning** : to go to the next page
**True** : real; genuine; authentic

Page 18. **Taught** : to learn something
**Tell** : to be able to understand a subject and express this
knowledge, to relate a story or information
**Time** :  the system of relations that any event has to any other,
as past, present, or future, indefinite and continuous duration
regarded as that in which events succeed one another
**Two** : a number
**Three** : a number

Page 19. **Then** : immediately or soon afterward
**Tired** : sleepy
**Tick-tock** : the sound a clock makes
**Nap time** : a short period for rest

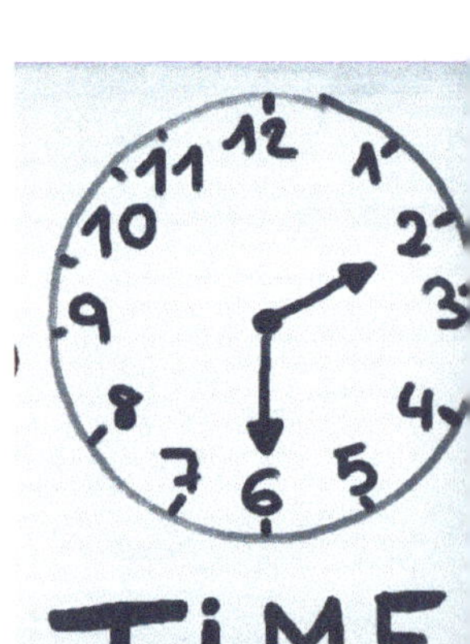


Page 20. **Thousand** : a large number
**Take-away** : math, subtraction on this page

Page 21. **Towers** : a unit of measure in math learning
**Totals** : the whole sum of something
**Thumbs** : the first finger on the hand

Page 22. **Thomas** : a boy or man's name
**Teenage** :  of the ages 13 to 19 years old
**Tarantula** : a large, hairy spider
**Tucked** : to put into a small, close, or concealing place
**Trouser** : a boy's pants

Page 23. **Tell** : to relate a story or information
**Tales** : stories sometimes made up or exaggerated ones
**Tackled** : to undertake to handle, master, solve,
**Toured** : a long journey including the visiting of a number of places in sequence, especially with an organized group led by a guide

 Page 24. **Tuneful** : nice music
**Tortoise** : a turtle
**Trombone** : a musical instrument

Page 25. **Tapir** : a large animal with a long, flexible snout/nose : all species are threatened or endangered
**Timpani** : a set of kettledrums used in an orchestra or band
**Tree frog** : a frog found in trees
**Telephone** :  an apparatus, system, or process for transmission of sound or speech to a distant point, especially by an electric device

Page 26. **Triangular** : something with three sides
**Tank** : a large receptacle, container, or structure for holding a liquid or gas:
**Tuna** : a sea fish
**Turbot** :  a flatfish
**Trout** : a fish

Page 27. **Teacher's aide:** an assistant to a teacher
**Tournado toboggan** : a large fast sled a long, narrow, flat-bottomed sled made of a thin board curved upward and backward at the front, often with low handrails on the sides, used especially in the sport of coasting over snow or ice
**Teddy** bears : soft stuffed bear toys

Page 28. **Twelve** : a number
**Tempted** : to attract, appeal strongly to, or invite
**Taste** : to try or test the flavor or quality of (something) by taking some into the mouth
**Tomatoes/Toast/Tacos/Tofu/Tandoori** : food

Page 29. **Take-away treats** : treats children take from school
**Tangerines** : fruit
**Tiramisu** : an Italian dessert with coffee and layers of sponge cake with custard and chocolate
**Tapioca** : a food prepared for puddings
**Tahini** : a flavorful sauce/paste made from sesame seeds
**Tap** : water from the kitchen faucet
**Tea** : a drink
**Tropical** juice : juice from a warm climate / area

Page 30. **Timetable** : a schedule for what to do next
**Tabards** : a loose outer garment, sleeveless or with short sleeves, especially one worn by a knight over his armor and usually emblazoned with his arms, a coarse, heavy, short coat, with or without sleeves, formerly worn outdoors
**Tan** : a color
**Turquoise** : a color
**Teal** (which is green) : a color
**Tahiti** : a country
**Texan** : a person from Texas, USA
**Thoroughbred** : a horse

Page 31. **Tapped** : to strike with a light but audible blow or blows; hit with repeated, slight blows
**Typewriter** : a machine for writing mechanically in letters and characters like those produced by printers
**Typing** : to write on a typewriter or keyboard
**Typed** : to write on a typewriter or keyboard
**Thomas** : a boy or man's name
**Tree** : a plant having a permanently woody main stem or trunk, ordinarily growing to a considerable height, and usually developing branches at some distance from the ground
**Top** : the highest point
**Teased** : to make a joke about someone
**Tasmanian Devil** : a small, predacious marsupial, *Sarcophilus harrisii*, of Tasmania, having a black coat with white patches: its dwindling population is now confined to isolated areas

Page 32. **Talent** : a special natural ability or aptitude
**Tremendous** : extraordinarily great in size, amount, or intensity or excellence
**Thanks** : an expression of appreciation or gratitude or an acknowledgment of services or favours given
**Things** : a material object without life or consciousness; an inanimate object

Page 33. **Trying** : something someone finds difficult
**Track** : to follow or pursue a track or trail
**Tricky** : given to or characterized by deceitful tricks, crafty; wily skilled in clever tricks or dodge
**Turning up** : to show up
**Term** : a period of time in school

Paula Curtis-Taylorson Lives in Marston Mortaine England. She is a full-time secondary school teacher of English and English Literature. She was amongst the first of the initial students to graduate from the UK's first BA (Hons) Creative Writing Program at the University of Bedfordshire.

Her first love is poetry and rhyme and she works hard to inspire and teach appreciation of the subject to all age groups. Many of her students have gone on to be successful writers.